THE WORLD'S CRAZIEST
ADULT
GAMES

summersdale

QUENTIN PARKER

THE WORLD'S CRAZIEST ADULT GAMES

Summersdale Publishers Ltd
46 West Street
Chichester
West Sussex
PO19 1RP
UK

www.summersdale.com

Printed and bound in Croatia

ISBN: 978-1-78685-076-8

Substantial discounts on bulk quantities of Summersdale books are available to corporations, professional associations and other organisations. For details contact general enquiries: telephone: +44 (0) 1243 771107, fax: +44 (0) 1243 786300 or email: enquiries@summersdale.com.

Disclaimer: The publisher urges care and caution in the pursuit of any of the activities represented in this book. This book is intended for use by adults only.

Have fun but play safe.

CONTENTS

INTRODUCTION

There's nothing better than getting together with friends or family for a special occasion, or even for no occasion at all, and playing your favourite games whilst sharing news and having lots of laughs. But sometimes as the party host, it's easy to go blank when it comes to thinking which game to play next or what the rules are, especially if you've had a few already. This book is the essential go-to for anyone looking to host a fun-filled evening and includes games of all shapes, sizes and nationalities.

For your convenience, each game is ranked out of three stars.

★ – the game is safe to play at a dinner party

★★ – it might be a bit wild

★★★ – these are the craziest games in the book where it's possible you might lose your dignity/break an ornament you forgot to move.

Each game is also given a theme that is represented by an icon:

Drinking

Card/Gambling

Sexy

Acting

Active/Sporty

Just Plain Weird

From drinking games to card games, sexy games to downright out-of-this-world games, *The World's Craziest Adult Games* will transform your parties into occasions your guests won't forget.

Life is more fun if you play games.

Roald Dahl

AMERICA

Craziness level: ★

Theme: 🂠

What you will need:

- 2–7 players
- Deck of cards, for 5 or fewer players; 2 decks of cards, for more than 5 players

HOW TO PLAY

Perfect for getting the family together

Each player starts with eight cards, or seven if there are only two players. Place the remaining cards in a stack face down on the middle of the table. The top card is turned over and play starts as the player to the dealer's left discards a card from their hand that is the same suit or same number as the previous card that was dealt. Play continues in this way, with the aim to be the first person to get rid of all their cards. If a player can't go, but they have a card bearing the number eight they can use this and announce a suit that the next player must put down. If the player doesn't have any of these cards, they must pick up one from the face-down deck. Once a player has got rid of all their cards, the other players must add up their scores. Eights score 50, court cards score ten and the other cards are scored at face value. These points are then passed to the winner. The overall winner is the person to score a total that is decided before the game. Usually this is 100 points for two players, 150 points for three, 200 for four, 250 for five, 300 for six and 350 for seven.

AMERICA

Strip-pong ←

Craziness level: ★★★

Theme: 👙🍺

What you will need:

- 2 or 4 players
- Table you don't mind playing on
- Regular and small cups
- Ping-pong balls
- A marker pen

First ping-pong, then beer-pong, now strip-pong (whatever next?)

Just like beer-pong apart from the bottoms of the cups are marked with the item of clothing the opposition must remove if you get the ball in. For those who aren't familiar with beer-pong, place six cups in a 3-2-1 triangle formation at either end of the table, with the line of three cups being nearest the edge of the table. Fill each cup with beer. You can either play in two teams of two, or one vs one. Each team stands at their end of the table and players take it in turns to throw a ping-pong ball into the opposing team's cups. If the ball lands in one of the cups, the other team must drink the contents of the cup, and flip it to see which item of clothing needs to be taken off.

Play continues until one team's cups have all been flipped over. They are the losers and must strip naked. Perhaps play a couple of games of beer-pong first to give yourselves some confidence.

It's never just
a game when
you're winning.

George Carlin

AMERICA

Find the Bubble Gum

Craziness level: ★★

Theme: 😎

What you will need:

- ◆ 2 or more players
- ◆ Bowls
- ◆ Bubble gum
- ◆ Aerosol whipped cream

Prepare to face the cream and dance

Line up your guests and give them each a bowl filled with whipped cream and a hidden unwrapped piece of bubble gum. Whoever finds the gum and blows a bubble first wins. The twist is they can only use their mouths.

ARMENIA

Egg Jousting ←

Craziness level: ★★

Theme:

What you will need:

- 2 players
- Coloured hard-boiled egg per player

The battle of the eggs

Each game starts with a defender and a challenger – these positions can be decided by playing a game of rock, paper, scissors, or tossing a coin.

The challenger must make one of four statements to the defender:

With my HEAD, I will break your HEEL.

With my HEEL, I will break your HEAD.

With my HEAD, I will break your HEAD.

With my HEEL, I will break your HEEL.

To accept the challenge, the defender replies 'Then break it' and cups the egg tightly in their hand with the relevant part of the egg (either the heel or the head) showing. The challenger then uses the part of the egg they declared they would use when making the statement to try to crack the defender's egg with. If they succeed in cracking the egg, the defender loses and must give up their egg as a sign of good sportsmanship. If the challenger doesn't manage to crack the egg, then the defender becomes the challenger in the next round. Rounds are played until an egg cracks.

AUSTRALIA

→ Toss the Thong

Craziness level: ★★

Theme: 🎳

What you will need:

- ◆ Group of players
- ◆ Flip flops
- ◆ Markers

**Knickers won't be
flying in this game**

In Australia, flip flops are called thongs and
because it is so darn hot there, thongs are
very popular and used in various ways. One of
these usages is precisely for this game. Gather
together as many flip flops/thongs as you
can and mark a line on the floor (preferably
somewhere outside) for contestants to stand
behind. One by one you each throw a flip flop/
thong as far as you can, then check where it
has landed and decide who the winner of the
round is. Before you start, decide how many
points you need to become the ultimate thong-
throwing winner.

?

DID YOU KNOW?

The largest toga party on record was held in Brisbane, Australia, where more than 3,700 people turned up.

AUSTRALIA

G'day, Bruce ←

Craziness level: ★

Theme:

What you will need:

- A group of people

Aussie accents are imperative

Players sit in a circle (the more people, the better) and everyone starts with the name Bruce. Play follows like so:

* Player one turns to their left and says 'G'day, Bruce'.

* This player (player two) returns the hello with another 'G'day, Bruce'.

* Player one then gestures to player three (the person to the left of player two) and says 'Say g'day to Bruce, Bruce'.

* Player two turns to player three and the game begins again around the circle, with player two saying 'G'day, Bruce'.

If a player makes a mistake or if they hesitate for too long, their name changes and play begins again starting with them. For the first mistake, their name changes to Shelia, then on their second mistake they become Harold, then Kylie, then Jason, then Lou, then Madge and by the seventh mistake that player is out of the game.

For example, if player one makes a mistake then play would continue like so:

- Player one turns to their left and says 'G'day, Bruce'.

- Player two returns the hello with 'G'day, Shelia'.

- Player one then gestures to player three and says 'Say g'day to Bruce, Bruce'.

CHILE

→ *Corre, Corre la Guaraca*

Craziness level: ★

Theme: 🏃 😶

What you will need:

- ◆ 5 or more players
- ◆ A handkerchief

When the handkerchief hits...

Players sit in a circle facing each other while one player runs around the perimeter. The players who are sitting must sing '*Corre, Corre, la Guaraca*, who looks back will be bopped on his head!' in unison and not look at what the standing player is doing. The standing player runs around the circle holding a handkerchief and chooses someone to drop it on as gently as possible. Once they drop it, the standing player must run around the circle and find their spot to sit down. If the person whom the handkerchief landed on doesn't notice what has happened before the runner sits down, they are out of the game. If they do catch on, they must try to catch the runner.

If they succeed in catching them, the runner is out, but if they don't, then play resumes with the seated player now becoming the standing player with the handkerchief. Players must run a full lap of the circle before they can sit down in their place. Play continues until players run out of steam.

ENGLAND

Centurion ←

Craziness level: ★★★

Theme: 🍺

What you will need:

- ◆ 2 or more players
- ◆ Beer (and lots of it)
- ◆ Shot glasses
- ◆ A watch

Training is necessary for this game

This game is simple but devastating. The only rule is to take a shot of beer every minute for 100 minutes. Have fun but don't be stupid. If you don't think you can last, sit out. Although the forfeit for admitting defeat is downing your drink (only joking!).

Beauty lies in the hands of the beer holder.

Anonymous

ENGLAND

→ Douche!

Craziness level: ★★

Theme: 🌀

What you will need:

- Group of players
- Egg cup
- Water
- Paper
- Pen

Save your bath or shower for the next day

Players sit in a circle and someone is nominated to be the doucher. The doucher calls out a category, such as 'cars', and writes down an example that they must not tell anyone else. The person to their left must think of an example in the category, such as 'BMW', and say it aloud. As this is happening, the doucher holds an egg cup with water in it over the person's head. If they say a different example to the doucher's, then they are safe and play continues. If they say the same example the doucher has written down, the doucher must show their answer and tip the water over the player's head. That player then becomes the doucher.

ENGLAND

→ **Ex Libris**

Craziness level: ★

Theme: 😨

What you will need:

- Group of players
- Book
- Paper
- Pens

Make sure your spelling is on point

Nominate someone to be the reader for this round. They choose a book (the more obscure the better) and read the first line out to the other players. Then the rest of the players have to guess what the last line of the book is, making sure it reflects the tone and style of the first line, and put their answers in a hat. The reader must write down the correct end line and pop that in the hat too. The reader then reads out the answers and the players must guess which is the real one. Players score one point for guessing correctly and one point for every time their line is chosen by another player. Once everyone has been the reader, you should add up the scores and see who is the winner.

ENGLAND

→ Wink Murder

Craziness level: ★★

Theme: 🎭

What you will need:

- A large group of people

Can you get away with the crime?

This game is best played with lots of people so it's harder to guess who is the murderer, but any more than 30 people and it starts to become confusing. You'll need a lot of space for this game so choose a suitable location before you play. A moderator is picked for the round. Everyone else sits down and closes their eyes and the moderator chooses a wink murderer by tapping the person's shoulder. Once the moderator has done this, everyone stands up and starts walking round the room, making general conversation. When passing other people, players must always make eye contact. If this happens and a player winks at you they are the murderer and have killed you. The player must not say anything but pretend to die – the more dramatic the better. Play continues in this way until someone thinks they know who the killer is. They shout 'I accuse' and raise their hand. For them to be able to guess, another person must shout 'I accuse' too. The first accuser gives their guess of who the wink murderer is and the accused must say if they are innocent or guilty. If guilty, the first accuser wins the game, but if innocent, the guess is given to the second accuser. If they are incorrect too, then both accusers leave the game and play continues. If the second accuser is correct, they win the game and a new round is started.

No one looks stupid when they are having fun.

Amy Poehler

FRANCE

→ Caps

Craziness level: ★

Theme:

What you will need:

- 2 players
- Beer bottles
- Beer bottle caps

HOW TO PLAY

An addictive drinking game. Probably not the best combination of words!

Two players sit apart from each other, each with a beer bottle and the bottle's cap placed upside down on top of it in front of them. Players take it in turns to knock the cap off their opponent's beer bottle by throwing spare bottle caps. (If you don't have any spare, it means you haven't drunk enough.) Fail and it's the other player's turn; win and the other player gets a chance to have another go at successfully hitting your cap off. If they don't then they must down half of their drink. If they do win the challenge, then you must play until someone fails.

FRANCE

→ Manille

Craziness level: ★

Theme: ♣♦

What you will need:

- 4 players
- Deck of cards

10s are the new aces in this game

This game requires 32 cards, including As, Ks, Qs, Js, 10s, 9s, 8s and 7s. Make teams of two and ensure you are sitting opposite each other. The cards are dealt equally between the players and the dealer chooses the trump suit, which can be any one of the suits, or no trump, where you can acquire double the points at the end of the game. If the dealer doesn't want to decide the trump, they can pass the decision to their partner. The opposing team can tap on the table if they think they can beat the chosen trump, i.e. score more than 30 points, as the total of cards equals 60. The scores of the cards rank like so:

- 10 – 5 points

- Ace – 4 points

- King – 3 points

- Queen – 2 points

- Jack – 1 point

- 9, 8 and 7 – 0 points

The player to the dealer's left plays a suit and the other three players must also play a card of the same suit. If they can't, a player can still win the hand by placing down a trump card. If they can't do either, the player must discard a card and by default they lose the round. The player who scores the most from that round starts the next round and the game continues until all 32 cards have been played. At the end, individuals calculate their scores and subtract them from 60, adding any doubles after this has been done. Then the players who are in a team add their scores together. If, for example, the winners score 36 and the losers 24, the winners would get six points, as you subtract 30 from their score, and the losers would score nothing. Play continues until a team scores 101 points.

DID YOU KNOW?

The King of Hearts is the only king in a deck of cards without a moustache.

GERMANY

Beer Stein Race ←

Craziness level: ★★★

Theme: 🍺🏃

What you will need:

- Group of people
- Beer
- Steins/mugs (to hold the beer)
- A bucket per contestant
- Obstacles (optional)

Try not to spill a drop!

This game is best played in a garden, park or field. Contestants line up in a row, holding as many beer-filled steins as they possibly can. The aim of the game is for the players to run from the start line to their bucket in the quickest time and without spilling the beer they are carrying. The losers are the contestants who have the least amount of beer in their bucket and ran the race in the slowest time. They then must down what's left in their bucket. If you want to make the game even more challenging, try adding obstacles to the course.

24 hours in a day, 24 beers in a case. Coincidence?

Steven Wright

GERMANY

→ *Topfschlagen* (Hit the Pot)

Craziness level: ★

Theme: 🏃 😊

What you will need:

- 2 or more players
- Individual chocolates or small counters
- Blindfold
- Small saucepan
- Wooden spoon or stick

Why the serious face?

Take the nominated player out of the room you are in and blindfold them so they can't see a thing when they go back in. In the meantime, someone else needs to put the saucepan upside-down in a hard-to-find place with the chocolate or counter inside it. Tell the player outside to come back in when you are ready and hand them the stick or wooden spoon. The aim of the game is for them to try to locate the saucepan and then bang on its bottom with the stick to announce they have found it. Their prize is what's underneath. If you choose to play with counters, these represent a forfeit that the winner of the challenge must give out.

To add an extra fun dimension to the game, decide on time limits to find the saucepan or hide multiple saucepans. If the contestant doesn't manage to find all the saucepans in the given time frame, then they have to do a forfeit themselves.

GERMANY

Bier Boot ←

Craziness level: ★

Theme: 🍺

What you will need:

- Group of people (preferably friends)
- Glass of beer

HOW TO PLAY

Sharing germs has never been such fun!

This is a very popular game that is played in Germany. A glass of beer is passed round a circle of friends (or strangers, if you dare) and each time it is passed the person being handed the beer must take a sip. The aim of the game is that the second-to-last person who takes a sip from the glass must pay for the next round of drinks. Although it sounds simple, tactical moves are often played so you have to prepare for your next turn in advance – do you take small sips or big gulps?

GERMANY

Mau Mau ←

Craziness level: ★

Theme: 🂠

What you will need:

• Traditional deck of cards

♦ 2 to 6 players

This is a game you want to lose to win

Players are dealt five cards each after choosing who goes first and the rest of the cards are placed face down in a stack. Play begins with the top card of the face-down deck being turned over and placed by the side of it, creating a discard pile. The aim of the game is to get rid of all your cards first and players take it in turns, going anticlockwise, to place a card on the discard pile. This card must either be the same number or suit as the last card that was placed on the pile. If you can't go, you must draw a card from the unused deck. Special cards also change the play of the game, for example:

Jack – changes the suit. A jack can't be followed by another jack.

9 – reverses the direction of play. For two players, play another card.

8 – skips a turn.

7 – the following player picks up two cards. If they are able to play a 7 the number of cards for the following player to pick up is doubled to four. If the following player also has a 7, then the next player must pick up eight.

Once you have discarded your second-to-last card you must say 'Mau' and you must say 'Mau Mau' before discarding your last card, otherwise you have to pick up a card.

?

In 1992, Bryan Berg was the first person to be given a Guinness World Record for the World's Tallest Card Tower. He turned his pastime into a career and has now managed to set a record of 25 feet and 3.5 inches, using 2,400 decks of playing cards to achieve this.

GHANA

Ampe ←

Craziness level: ★★

Theme: 😶

What you will need:

- ◆ 4 or more players (though 2 people can play)
- ◆ Plenty of space to jump around in

Put your best foot forward

Have you ever played rock, paper, scissors – with your feet? This traditional game from Ghana will let you do just that.

To play in pairs, line everyone up facing each other, and nominate one side to be 'leaders'. Everybody jumps at the same time and claps twice. On the second clap, when they land, each person puts one leg forward. If the leader and the facing player have the same foot forward (i.e. both right or both left – this is called 'bend'), the leader gains a point. If they land with opposite feet facing forward (this is called 'straight'), the other player becomes the leader. The play continues, and usually the first person to reach ten points wins!

You can also play with two teams lined up facing one another. Start with one person from each team jumping and clapping together. The person who wins that point moves on to challenge the next person in the facing team, and play carries on until all the players in one team have been beaten. At this point, the victorious team chooses a player from the losing team to leave the game. The winning team is the one that succeeds in ejecting all the players from their rival team. By the time you finish, everyone will be hot and bothered – and you'll see the competitive side come out in even your quietest friends!

?

DID YOU KNOW?

Ghana produces the second most cocoa beans in the world, after Ivory Coast. But even though Ghanaian chocolate is delicious, we don't recommend eating too much before you play Ampe – you might live to regret it!

GHANA

Pilolo ←

Craziness level: ★★

Theme:

What you will need:

- A field or woods
- Distinguishable objects, e.g. brightly coloured clothing, sports equipment and household items
- At least 5 players

Find and run

This game requires a timekeeper, a leader and some players. It is best played outdoors. The timekeeper stands at the finish line of the course and the leader hides the distinguishable objects within the vicinity of the course for the players to find. The players will study the items in advance to know what they are looking for. The winner is the person who finds the most objects and runs across the finish line in the quickest time.

IRELAND

Shot Potato ←

Craziness level: ★★

Theme: 🍺

What you will need:

- Group of players
- A potato
- Music

One potato, two potato, three potato, four

Players sit in a circle with one person in control of stopping and starting the music. A potato is passed around the rest of the players while music plays and once it stops the player holding the potato must down a shot. Play can last however long you want it to as there are no winners, as such, just some people will get more drunk than others!

When life gives you lemons, you make lemonade – and then try to find someone whose life is giving them vodka.

Ron White

IRELAND

→ Irish Poker

Craziness level: ★

Theme: 🂡🍺

What you will need:

- ♦ 2 or more players
- ♦ Deck of cards

Not for the faint-hearted

Players sit in a circle and four cards are dealt face down in a row to each player. Not looking at the cards, the player to the dealer's left must guess if the card on the far left of their row will be red or black. If they are correct then they choose another player to drink two gulps but if they are incorrect they must take two gulps. Play continues around the circle until all the far-left cards on the table have been played. The players must then guess whether the second card in their line is higher or lower than the first, whether the third is in-between or outside of the other two cards and the fourth the player must guess the suit.

IRELAND

→ Road Bowling

Craziness level: ★★★

Theme: 🏃

What you will need:

- 2 teams of players
- Quiet, winding lane
- Metal ball

Don't get lost!

Players work in teams to throw their ball over the finish line first. You need to find a lane that is winding and not used much. Also, take into account if there are houses on either side of the lane as you wouldn't want to pay for inadvertently throwing a ball through a window. Mark where the start and finish line will be before play commences, making sure the lane is long enough for the game to last a good length of time. Decide which team throws first with a simple game of rock, paper, scissors.

Players take it in turns to throw the ball and the rest of the team can assist the player with advice on which direction to throw the ball around blind spots of the lane. Choose a muddy lane so that the ball is less likely to bounce. If the team loses their ball, they must go back to the last place it was thrown.

ISRAEL

Go-Go-Im ←

Craziness level: ★

Theme: 😊

What you will need:

- 2 or more players
- At least 20 apricot pits per player. Alternatively you can use any soft fruit stones, small stones or acorns
- A shoebox per player

Who could have known apricot pits would be so fun?

Prepare the game by cutting six holes of various sizes out of the shoebox lid. If you are very competitive, create six templates first so that you know that each hole will be the same size as the holes in the other players' shoeboxes. At least one of the holes should be just bigger than the apricot pits. Next to each hole, write down a value. Place the shoeboxes on the ground and make sure the players are standing in a line approximately five feet away from the shoeboxes. Players take it in turns to throw the pits into the shoeboxes' holes. If they manage to score in their own shoebox they are awarded the points next to the respective hole. If they choose and succeed in throwing their stone in another player's shoebox, then the points are doubled. Before you play, decide on how many points you need to become the winner.

?

Alexander the Great has been said to have made the biggest party blooper of all time. After conquering Persia, he celebrated by throwing a party. However, the drinking got out of hand and he managed to burn down the city palace, which he had just taken possession of.

ITALY

Briscola ←

Craziness level: ★

Theme:

What you will need:

- Deck of cards
- 2 to 5 players

Three is the magic number

Remove the jokers, eights, nines and tens from a 52-card deck. Trick points are as follows:

Ace – 11 points

Three – 10 points

King – 4 points

Queen – 3 points

Jack – 2 Points

Anything else – 0 points

The dealer gives each player three cards and then turns the next card face up from the remaining pile of cards. This card determines the briscola suit. Place the rest of the cards face down, half covering the trump card, and game commences in an anticlockwise direction. The player to the right of the dealer plays a card, which doesn't necessarily need to match the suit of the trump card, and the other players follow. If a trump card is played, the highest trump wins the trick. If a trump card isn't played, then the highest card of the suit that begun the trick wins. The trick winner picks up the top card from the deck and other players do the same. Play continues until the deck is gone, including the trump card which was determined at the beginning of the game. The winner is the person whose tricks contain the most points.

If winning isn't everything, why do they keep score?

Vince Lombardi

ITALY

Lupo Mangia Frutta ←

Craziness level: ★★

Theme: 🏃 😀

What you will need:

- ◆ Group of people

There's always one hungry wolf at the party

Go back to your halcyon days of childhood with this Italian game that links fruit and hungry wolves. One person is chosen to be the wolf and the other players pretend to be types of fruit. Acting out the fruit is a requirement but you must also shout out which fruit you are before the game starts to avoid any confusion. Players stand in a group and call out 'Which fruit do you want?' to the wolf. The wolf names one, and the person he has chosen must run from the safety of the pack to a safety zone that is chosen before the game begins. If that person is captured by the wolf, they then become the wolf.

ITALY

P'zz'cantò ←

Craziness level: ★★★

Theme: 🏃 🙂

What you will need:

- ◆ 6 to 13 people

One slip and you could all come tumbling down

This should only be attempted by those who are healthy and without injury. The floor should be padded or soft to lessen the impact of a fall, if this does happen. Team work is essential for the success of this game and the aim is to build a human tower. The human tower should be two or three levels and be free to move, unlike the traditional human pyramid. The people forming the top levels of the tower can either stand or sit on the shoulders of the people on the bottom level. Once you have made your tower, the aim is to travel 100 metres from your starting point, singing and moving in rhythm to Italian music.

?

DID YOU KNOW?

**The first stag parties were invented
by Spartan soldiers in ancient Greece.
The night before the wedding, the
Spartans would eat, drink and
gamble the night away to mark the
groom's last day of bachelorhood.**

ITALY

→ *Corsa Con la Cannata*

Craziness level: ★★★

Theme: 🏃 😀

What you will need:

- Earthenware pot
- A stretch of cloth (a tea towel would do the trick)
- Water
- 4 or more players

**A running race
with a twist**

Originally, this Italian game was exclusively intended for women, but I'm sure, for the purposes of this book, we can include men too. Players are in teams of two and the winners are the contestants who run the race in the quickest time. The first contestants run to a halfway point in the race where the second contestants are waiting. The second players complete the second half of the race and finish by returning to where the first racers started from. Although this sounds like a simple running race, it's not.

Whilst running, you must balance an earthenware pot (called a *cannata* in Italian) filled with water on your head and pass it to your teammate once you've finished your part of the course. To aid balancing the pot on your head, cloths are rolled up to form a donut shape on which you can position the *cannata*.

?

Launched in September 2003, an international festival of traditional games, Tocatì, is held in Verona, Italy, to give residents and tourists a feel-good vibe in a month that can bring about melancholy. It runs over three days and offers the public the chance to take part in or spectate a variety of games from around the world.

JAPAN

→ *Butanoshippo*

Craziness level: ★

Theme: 🃏

What you will need:

- Deck of cards
- 3 or more players

Quick reaction speeds are essential

With a full pack of face-down cards, make a circle. Players get ready by placing one of their hands outside the circle. Do rock, paper, scissors to decide the order of play. Sticking to the order, each player picks up a card from the circle, flips it to face upwards, puts it inside the circle and places their hand back outside the circle. This continues until someone flips over an attack card, which can be a joker, or a card of the same suit or of the same number as the card that's just been flipped. When this happens, all players must put their hands on the attack card and the person with their hand on the top of the pile must take all the cards that are inside the ring. The loser is the person with the most cards at the end of the game.

Play is the highest form of research.

Albert Einstein

JAPAN

Kiku No Hana ←

Craziness level: ★★

Theme: 😳

What you will need:

- ◆ Small piece of sponge
- ◆ 3 identical plastic cups
- ◆ Alcohol
- ◆ 2 to 4 players

Which cup will it be?

You probably still have this in your loft somewhere from when you used to do magic tricks as a child. The dealer places one sponge under one of the three cups and moves the cups around in front of the players. Players must guess which cup the sponge is in. However, in this game, if the player guesses correctly they must pour alcohol into the other two cups and down them.

JAPAN

Sumo

Craziness level: ★★★

Theme: 🏃 😵

What you will need:

- Teeny tiny pants
- 2 or more players

Does my bum look big in this?

Attempt to play this contact sport with friends to see who is the better sumo wrestler. Play on a soft surface and mark out where the ring stops. Everyone must be dressed for the occasion in their best sumo knickers. The aim of the game is to push the other contestant out of the ring without touching the ground with anything but your feet.

?

DID YOU KNOW?

In order to maintain their weight, sumo wrestlers must eat a huge amount of food each day. Every morning they skip breakfast for training so that their metabolism slows down for the rest of the day. Then they gorge on a protein-rich meal for lunch, with the aim to keep eating until they are almost physically sick. This is followed by a nap, so that calories are preserved, and then another round of feasting in the evening.

MEXICO

→ Dudo

Craziness level: ★★

Theme: 🍺

What you will need:

- Dice – however many you choose; the more dice, the more challenging
- A cup
- 3 or more people

Liar, liar, pants on fire!

This game is usually played with five dice. But it is completely up to you – or dependent on how many dice you have lying around the house. Take it in turns to be the roller. The roller puts the dice in a cup and shakes it, then takes a look inside and announces how many of the dice have rolled the same number (for example, five sixes). It is up to the roller to decide if they want to lie or not – the higher the number of same-number dice, the more fingers each penalty drink is worth. The rest of the players then each state whether they think the roller has lied or not.

If one of them says that the roller has lied and the roller is indeed found to have been telling a fib, then the roller has to take a drink (in this case, it would be five fingers' worth). However, if the roller was telling the truth, then the player to call them a liar takes a drink (again, of five fingers).

Creativity is intelligence having fun.

Albert Einstein

MEXICO

→ Eating Challenge

Craziness level: ★★★

Theme: 😶

What you will need:

- Spicy food
- Milk (for when things get too spicy)
- 2 or more players

How much can you handle?

Challenge your friends to a Mexican-themed eating contest. Buy supplies of nachos and chillies and have competitions of who can eat the most of the respective foods in a certain time without taking a drink. One-on-one challenges are often the most fun as spectators can cheer on the contestant they want to win. You could even start a betting system. Make sure you have enough milk for players to gulp down once the game has finished.

MEXICO

→ **Pass the Sombrero**

Craziness level: ★★

Theme: 🙃

What you will need:

- A sombrero
- 2 teams of players

Try not to strain your neck

Players form two teams and create two lines. The sombrero must be passed from the front of the line to the back in the quickest time. The first pass must be made chin to chin, the second pass is made between the legs and so on, similar to the game Pass the Orange. You can make the passes as creative as you like, but must make sure everyone knows the sequence before the game starts. If someone in your team drops the sombrero, then you must start from the beginning again.

THE NETHERLANDS

→ *Piramidespel*

Craziness level: ★★

Theme: 🃏🍺

What you will need:

- 3 or more players
- A deck of playing cards

Can you get to the top of the pyramid?

This is a game of deception: your main aim is to make your opponents drink more than you. The game begins by laying out a face-down pyramid of cards on the table, usually six cards at the base, then five above that, then four, and so on. Each player is then dealt three cards. Each player can only look and memorise these cards once before the game has begun. These cards must be kept a secret from everyone else.

Starting at the bottom left of the pyramid and playing left to right, bottom to top, each player turns over a card; if a player claims to have a card of the same face value, then they can nominate someone else to drink. The player told to drink can either do so or they can call the nominating player's bluff. If the nominating player was lying, then they must take a drink. If they were not lying, however, the original victim has to drink double.

Each card that is revealed is replaced by a new one from the deck.

I knew I was drunk: I felt sophisticated and couldn't pronounce it.

Anonymous

NORWAY

→ **Commando Bimbaloh**

Craziness level: ★★

Theme: 🍺

What you will need:

• 3 or more players

Attention!

One person is chosen as the commander; they will call out commands. The commands are as follows:

'COMMANDO BIMBALOH' is the command for everyone to drum their fingers on the table, as if mimicking a drum roll.

'COMMANDO KANT' is the command for everyone to do a karate chop with both hands.

'COMMANDO STOH' is the command for everyone to place their fingertips on the table, arching their palms like crabs. Both hands should be used, 20 cm apart from each other.

'COMMANDO DOUBLE STOH' is the command for everyone to place their crabs one on top of the other.

If the commander calls out 'BIMBALOH,' 'KANT,' 'STOH' or 'DOUBLE STOH' without the preceding 'COMMANDO' you mustn't perform any command.

If any player makes a mistake they should drink!

PAKISTAN

Oonch Neech ←

Craziness level: ★★

Theme: 🏃 🙂

What you will need:

- A large, open space
- A group of people

Run, run, as fast as you can

Choose one player to be the chaser. They count to five while the other players try their best to run away. The game is similar to the British game It, however, if a player finds a place to stand that is higher than ground level, for example, a rock, a tree stump or a branch of a tree, then this player is safe while they remain in that spot. To make the game more challenging, make a rule where players can't stay in safe areas for more than ten seconds.

Just keep taking chances and having fun.

Garth Brooks

RUSSIA

→ Mafia

Craziness level: ★

Theme: 🏃 😈

What you will need:

- At least 7 players
- Deck of cards

Goodies vs Baddies

There are two teams: the mafia and the innocents; and six roles: one moderator, two members of the mafia, two members of the police, one doctor and the rest of the players are townspeople. Each player is assigned an identity by picking a card from the moderator at the beginning of the game. For example, two aces could represent the mafia, two kings could represent the police and so on.

Role goals:

Mafia – protect their identities as mafia members and try to eliminate as many townspeople as possible

Police – determine who is a member of the mafia and who isn't and help the townspeople decide the elimination correctly

Doctor – try to protect people during the night phase

Townspeople – determine Mafia members and eliminate them during the day phase

Players sit in a circle and the moderator stands. The moderator acts as narrator and takes the players through each phase of the game. The first is night-time and the moderator tells everyone to go to sleep (in other words, players put their heads down and close their eyes). Then, the moderator tells the mafia to wake up and point to a person they want to eliminate from the game. The moderator tells the mafia to go to sleep and asks the police to wake up. The police then silently guess by pointing who they think is a member of the mafia. The moderator nods or shakes their head to let the police know if they are correct. The police are told to go to sleep and the doctor is asked to wake up. The doctor points to a person who he would like to protect and then goes back to sleep until the moderator notifies all the players that it is daytime and they must wake up.

In the daytime phase of the game, the moderator announces who is eliminated, unless the doctor guessed the mafia's decision correctly. The person who is out of the game must leave the circle. The townspeople, including the mafia and police who can feign identities as townspeople, must discuss and vote on a person whom they think is in the mafia. The accused can defend themselves and plead their case. To eliminate someone, there must be a majority vote (50 per cent or over). Once the vote has been made, the daytime phase is over and the night-time phase begins again.

The winners are those who successfully eliminate all their opponents.

RUSSIA

Tactical Manoeuvres ←

Craziness level: ★★★

Theme: 🏃 😵

What you will need:

- ♦ Blindfolds
- ♦ Water balloons or soft balls

It's a minefield out there

This game requires two teams. One player from each team must walk/run blindfolded from one point to another without stepping on the obstacles in their way, which could be water balloons or soft balls. The idea is for players to finish before their opponent and not step on the obstacles. Directions can be given by their teammates. The team with the most players left at the end wins.

Sometimes the only way to stay sane is to go a little crazy.

Matt Nguyen

RUSSIA

→ *Verish' Ne Verish'*

Craziness level: ★

Theme: 🂡

What you will need:

- 4–6 players
- Deck of cards

Trust or don't trust

Using 52 cards, the dealer asks a player to pick one card at random and put it face down to the side of play. The rest of the cards are dealt to players one at a time in a clockwise rotation. The player to the left of the dealer begins by putting one, two or three cards face down on the table and names a rank (e.g. 5s), which could be different to the cards they have put down. There are two moves the next player can make:

1. They can say 'I trust' and add one, two or three cards to the pile on the table, repeating aloud the same rank that was declared by the previous player.

2. They can say 'I don't trust', to which the previous player must expose their cards. If the accuser is correct and the rank of the cards differed from what they said, then the accused must pick up all the cards on the table and the accuser starts the next round. If the accuser is incorrect, they must pick up the cards and the player to the left of them starts a new round.

Play continues with the aim to get rid of your cards before anyone else. If you have four cards of the same rank, these can be removed from your hand and put on the pile of cards in the middle before you take your go. The loser is the last player to have cards.

SPAIN

Burro ←

Craziness level: ★

Theme: 🃏

What you will need:

- ◆ Deck of cards
- ◆ 4–8 players

Don't be the ass (or *burro* if you're Spanish)

Spanish playing cards are traditionally used in this game, but English playing cards are just as good. The aim of the game is to get four of the same number before the other players do. Before you begin the game, sort out the cards so that you have four cards in each suit for each person who is playing. For example, if four people are playing then you would need four cards from four ranks, which would equal 16 cards in total. All players discard an unwanted card and give it to the person on their left. This should happen quickly to keep the game lively. Once someone has four cards of the same rank they must lay down their hand as quickly as possible, and the other players need to put their cards down too. The player who puts down their hand last is the *burro*.

?

DID YOU KNOW?

It is said that China was the first country to invent playing cards around the ninth century. Previously, they had played games such as Dominos with bone or ivory tiles but these were replaced by the bendier paper playing cards.

SPAIN

→ *Chapas*

Craziness level: ★★

Theme: 🙂

What you will need:

* Bottle caps
* Chalk

HOW TO PLAY

Simple but addictive

You need different branded or coloured bottle caps for this game. Each player picks a bottle cap and two parallel lines are drawn with chalk, the ends of which mark the start and finish lines. Players must take it in turns to flick their bottle caps, making sure they don't go outside the lines. If they do, they must start from the beginning. The player who crosses the finish line with their bottle cap first is the winner.

Life is too important to be taken seriously.

Oscar Wilde

SPAIN

Churro, Mediamanga, Mangotero ←

Craziness level: ★★★

Theme: 🙂

What you will need:

- ◆ 2 teams

(4 to 8 players in each team)

Release your inner child

One team lines up in a row, each player in a crouched position putting their head in between the legs of the person in front of them. The first person in the line stands upright with their back against a wall or tree and holds the second person's head in their hands. The other team must aim to get all their players on the backs of the first team by leapfrogging as far as possible without falling off. If any of the jumpers fall off or if the team crouched collapse in the process the teams must start again. Once all the team have secured themselves on the backs of the other team, the first jumper must ask the question '*Churro, mediamanga, mangotero, guess what*

comes first?' and put their right hand on top of their left hand (churro), their right hand on their left wrist (manga) or their right hand on their left shoulder (mango). The crouching team must then guess what the first jumper has chosen. If they are correct, the teams swap positions.

Good parties create a temporary youthfulness.

Mason Cooley

SPAIN

Los Chunguitos ←

Craziness level: ★★

Theme: 🍺

What you will need:

- Alcohol
- Los Chunguitos music
- Group of people

Completely bonkers!

Play your favourite Los Chunguitos song – if you haven't a clue who this band is then choose one of their songs at random. Players must sit in a circle and start clapping to the beat. Then each person around the circle must call a number, starting from one. The person who is number one must say their number and another player's, then the person whose number was called out repeats the process saying their number followed by someone else's. Simultaneously, the person sitting to the right of the person whose number was called out must think of an instrument and imitate it. As soon as someone forgets to add an instrument sound, they must take two gulps of their drink and the game restarts.

?

DID YOU KNOW?

Buñol, Spain, holds a festival every year called La Tomatina, in which the public throw tomatoes at each other. At least 100 tonnes of tomatoes are used in this celebration.

ZIMBABWE

→ Kudoda

Craziness level: ★

Theme: 😎

What you will need:

- A bowl
- Marbles
- 2 or more players

Harder than it sounds

Players form a circle with a bowl of marbles in the middle. Each player takes turns throwing a marble and picking up as many marbles as they can from the bowl while it is still in the air. If they don't catch the marble that they threw, they must put all the marbles they collected back in the bowl. Play continues until all the marbles in the bowl have gone. The person who collected the most marbles is the winner.

A playful path is the shortest road to happiness.

Bernie DeKoven

WORLDWIDE

Travel the World ←

Craziness level: ★

Theme:

What you will need:

- Group of people

You don't need to be good at geography to play this

Players sit in a circle and someone calls out a country beginning with 'T'. The person to their left then calls out a country beginning with 'R'. Play continues and the aim of the game is to spell 'travel the world' by saying countries' names that begin with the respective letter. If someone hesitates, they must drink two sips and the game restarts with the person to their left. Country names cannot be repeated in a round.

If you're interested in finding out
more about our books, find us on
Facebook at Summersdale Publishers and
follow us on Twitter at @Summersdale.

www.summersdale.com